7/2014

y

W9-BZV-288

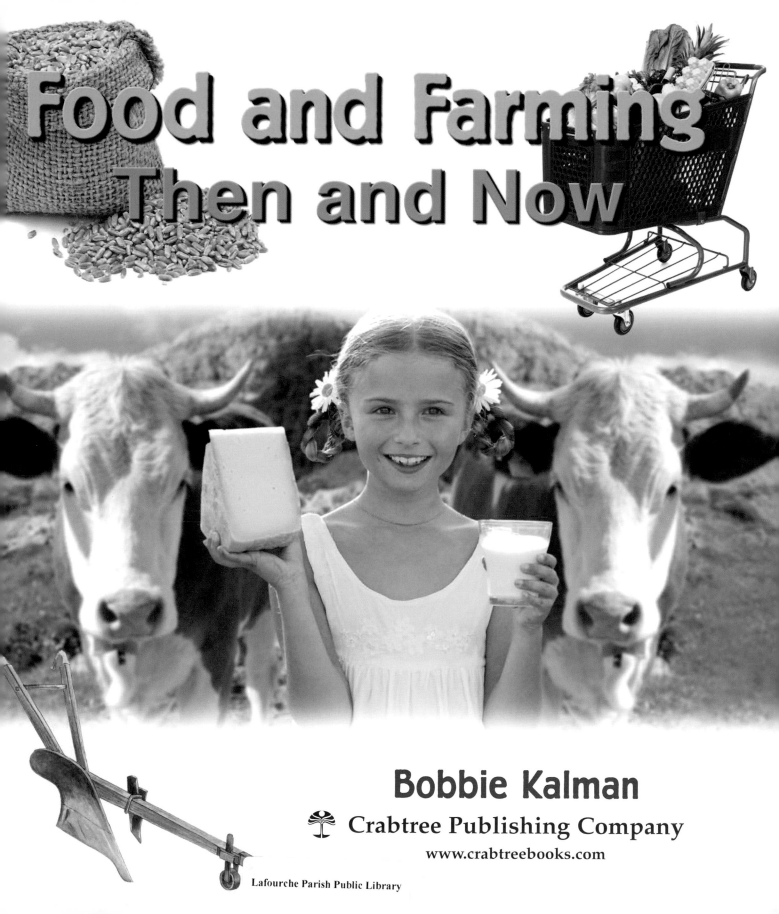

Food and Farming
Then and Now

Bobbie Kalman

Crabtree Publishing Company

www.crabtreebooks.com

Created by Bobbie Kalman

For Henriett Halasz,
with love from your cousin
across the ocean

Author and Editor-in-Chief
Bobbie Kalman

Editors
Kathy Middleton
Crystal Sikkens

Photo research
Bobbie Kalman

Design
Bobbie Kalman
Samantha Crabtree
Katherine Berti
Samara Parent (front cover)

Prepress technician
Katherine Berti

Print coordinator
Margaret Amy Salter

Illustrations and reproductions
Barbara Bedell: front and back cover, pages 1, 3, 5, 7, 9,
    13, 15, 17, 19 (bottom left and right), 21
Antoinette "Cookie" Bortolon: page 19 (middle left)
Wikimedia Commons: John George Brown: cover
    (middle right), page 11 (top)

Photographs
Thinkstock: page 4 (right), 6 (inset), 11 (bottom),
    12 (top left), 20 (top right)
Other images by Shutterstock, as well as cover photographs

Library and Archives Canada Cataloguing in Publication

Kalman, Bobbie, author
     Food and farming then and now / Bobbie Kalman.

(From olden days to modern ways in your community)
Includes index.
Issued in print and electronic formats.
ISBN 978-0-7787-0126-2 (bound).--ISBN 978-0-7787-0208-5 (pbk.).
--ISBN 978-1-4271-9415-2 (pdf).--ISBN 978-1-4271-9409-1 (html)

     1. Agriculture--Juvenile literature. 2. Food--Juvenile
literature. I. Title.

S519.K35 2013   j338.1   C2013-906080-4
                                       C2013-906081-2

Library of Congress Cataloging-in-Publication Data

Kalman, Bobbie.
  Food and farming then and now / Bobbie Kalman.
       pages cm -- (From olden days to modern ways in your community)
  Includes index.
  Audience: 5-8
  Audience: K to grade 3
  ISBN 978-0-7787-0126-2 (reinforced library binding) -- ISBN 978-0-7787-0208-5 (pbk.)
  -- ISBN 978-1-4271-9415-2 (electronic pdf) -- ISBN 978-1-4271-9409-1 (electronic html)
  1. Agriculture--Juvenile literature. 2. Food--Juvenile literature. 3. Farms--Juvenile
literature. 4. Farms, Small--Juvenile literature. I. Title. II. Series: Kalman, Bobbie.
From olden days to modern ways in your community.

S519.K358 2013
630--dc23
                                       2013034928

Crabtree Publishing Company
www.crabtreebooks.com   1-800-387-7650

Printed in Canada/012014/BF20131120

Published in Canada
Crabtree Publishing
616 Welland Ave.
St. Catharines, Ontario
L2M 5V6

Published in the United States
Crabtree Publishing
PMB 59051
350 Fifth Avenue, 59th Floor
New York, New York 10118

Published in the United Kingdom
Crabtree Publishing
Maritime House
Basin Road North, Hove
BN41 1WR

Published in Australia
Crabtree Publishing
3 Charles Street
Coburg North
VIC 3058

What is in this book?

How do we get our food?

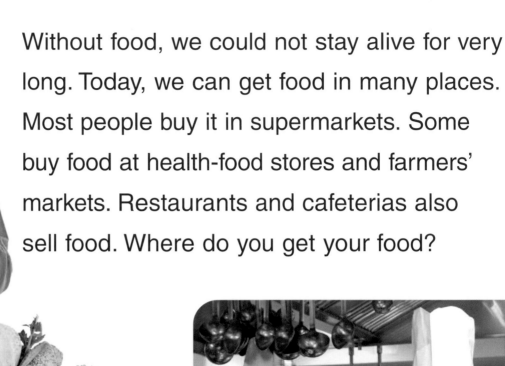

Without food, we could not stay alive for very long. Today, we can get food in many places. Most people buy it in supermarkets. Some buy food at health-food stores and farmers' markets. Restaurants and cafeterias also sell food. Where do you get your food?

Many people today eat in restaurants. This chef prepares delicious dishes.

Where did people long ago buy food?

In the old days, there were not many places to buy food. There were no supermarkets and very few restaurants. Most people grew their own food. They could also go to a **general store** and **barter**, or trade, some of the foods they grew for foods they did not grow. The general store also sold other things people needed.

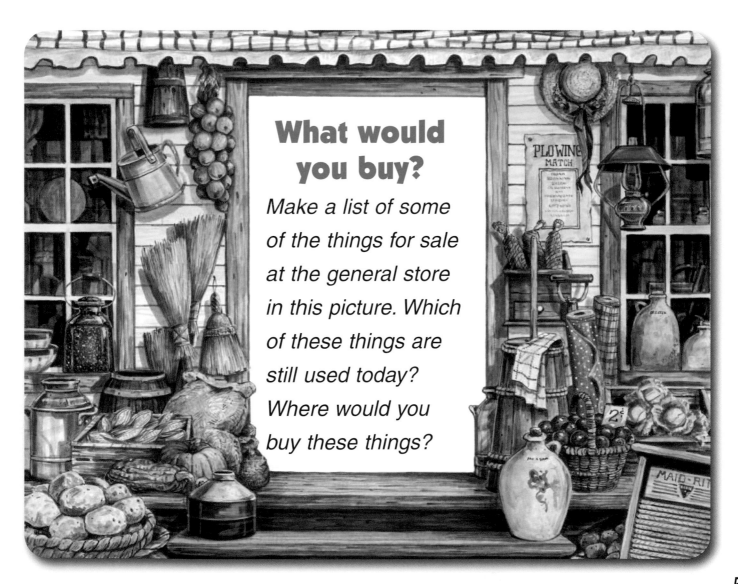

What would you buy?

Make a list of some of the things for sale at the general store in this picture. Which of these things are still used today? Where would you buy these things?

Farming then and now

canola
flower

canola
oil

seeds

Today, some people grow their own food, but most of our food comes from huge farms. The farms either grow **crops** or raise animals. The foods they grow or raise are made into different kinds of **products**. Many of the products are **processed**. Processed foods are put into packages or cans and have added **ingredients** to keep them from going bad.

This modern farm grows canola in huge fields like this one. The seeds are made into oil and other products.

Packaged foods are sold in stores.

BRAN FLAKES

Starting a farm long ago

Long ago, when people arrived in a new area, they built a home and planted some crops so their families would have food to eat. Farmers helped one another by sharing some crops or exchanging seeds to grow new crops. The animals they raised were kept in barns. To build barns, many farmers held barn-raising **bees**. Bees were work parties.

Neighbors helped one another build barns at barn-raising bees. When the work was finished, everyone enjoyed a huge meal, music, and fun.

7

Food from grains

wheat field

combine harvester

In most countries, bread is a **staple food**. A staple food is eaten every day. Bread comes from **grains** such as wheat, oats, and rye. Today, these grains are grown in huge fields and are cut down by machines called **combine harvesters**. The grain is ground into flour and packaged in factories. Some of it is used to make bread, pasta, cereals, and cakes, which are sold in stores.

Bread and pasta are made from wheat and other grains.

Which grains?

Wheat, oats, rye, corn, and barley are all grains. Name some foods you eat that are made from these grains.

From grain to flour

Long ago, people ate bread every day, just as we do today. There were no machines in those days, so farmers cut down the wheat and corn they grew by hand. They used simple tools, such as **scythes** and **sickles**, shown on the right (see also page 17).

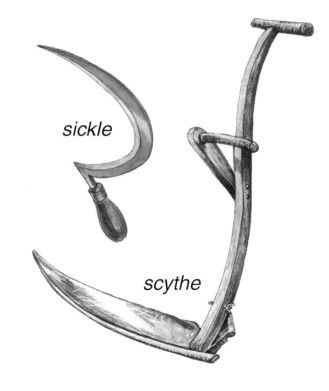

sickle

scythe

windmill

flour

wheat

grain

Wheat was ground into flour at **gristmills**. The grinding stone in this gristmill was powered by a windmill.

This woman uses flour to make bread and cakes.

Vegetables and fruit

This girl is picking lettuce grown in her family's garden.

Vegetables are great for us! They are plant foods that grow in soil or in water. Fruits also grow in soil, as well as on trees. Most people today buy their fruits and vegetables at supermarkets, but many families grow their own vegetables or buy them at **local** markets. Local markets are close to home.

This girl and her mother buy apples at a supermarket.

Close to home

If you cannot grow a garden at your home, ask your parents to visit a farmers' market nearby.

Home-grown foods

Long ago, most people grew their own vegetable gardens and even had fruit trees, such as apple, cherry, and peach. People ate some of the fruits and vegetables they grew. They also **preserved** some and traded some at the general store.

These children are eating some of the apples that were picked to make **cider** at their family's farm.

People grew vegetables such as lettuce, potatoes, cucumbers, and pumpkins.

Honey and syrup

Bees collect nectar from flowers.

Bees make honey from the nectar in flowers. They store the honey in their hives.

Beekeepers keep bees in human-made hives.

Sugar was not easy to get long ago, so people sweetened their foods with honey or maple syrup. We get these foods today in the same way that farmers did long ago.

Collecting honey

Bees fly from flower to flower to collect **nectar**. Their bodies make the nectar into honey, which the bees use for food. Early settlers used to follow bees to find their hives and collect the honey stored inside. They also learned how to raise bees to make honey. People today still keep bees so they can use their honey.

Maple syrup

Maple syrup also comes from plants. It is made from the sweet **sap**, or liquid, inside maple trees. Maple sap drips out of a maple tree into a pail through a spout. The sap is boiled until it becomes a thick syrup.

Did you know?

Pure honey and maple syrup do not spoil if their containers have not been opened. Honey has been found that is thousands of years old.

Making maple syrup long ago was not very different from how it is made today. The sap was collected in huge barrels and boiled in big kettles over a fire.

Food from animals

Milk and cheese come from cows.

Meat, eggs, milk, and cheese are all foods that come from animals. In the past, people hunted many of the animals they ate. Today, we get meat from animals such as pigs, chickens, turkeys, and cattle. Most **livestock**, or farm animals, are raised in huge barns. Farmers today have many machines to help them look after the livestock.

Chickens lay eggs. These eggs came from **free-range** chickens.

Some farmers raise their animals free range, the way it was done long ago. Free-range animals are allowed to roam free.

Animal foods long ago

The first settlers in North America ate whatever meat they could find. They hunted wild rabbits, deer, and pigeons, which lived all around them. They also raised some livestock for their meat, eggs, and milk. In the West, cattle were raised on huge ranches on which cowboys lived and worked. Part of their job was to round up these animals and take them to towns that had train stations. The cattle were then **transported**, or carried, by train to cities in the East, where people bought their meat.

There was no refrigeration, so cowboys had to herd the cattle live to railway stations. The cowboys worked hard to keep the cattle together and not lose any along the way.

Farming tools

New farm machines do the work once done by many farm workers.

Today, farming is done with the help of machines and computers. Computers make it easy for farmers to get weather forecasts, find out which plants grow better in which season, and learn new ways of farming.

These cows are hooked up to a computer-controlled milking system. Automatic milking gives farmers more time to look after their farms and cows.

Simple tools

Running a farm long ago was hard work. Farmers did not have big machines or computers to help them. They used simple tools and animal power to plant and harvest crops. Many made their own tools.

These farmers are using scythes to cut down hay. They pile it onto a wagon.

Cows were milked by hand.

*Farmers used horses to help them **till** the ground, or prepare it for planting crops.*

Kitchen tools

Today, we have many kinds of **appliances** for preparing food. We cook and bake using stoves, ovens, microwaves, and barbecues. We also use small appliances, such as blenders, waffle irons, toasters, and juicers. Make a list of the appliances and cookware that your family uses to prepare food.

toaster

blender

waffle iron

This family loves having barbecues!

juicer

18

Cooking long ago

Before electricity, people cooked their food over a fire in a fireplace. Just as we have many cooking tools today, kitchens long ago also had many, but those tools were not powered by electricity.

Do you know?

Why was cooking long ago more dangerous than it is today? See the picture below.

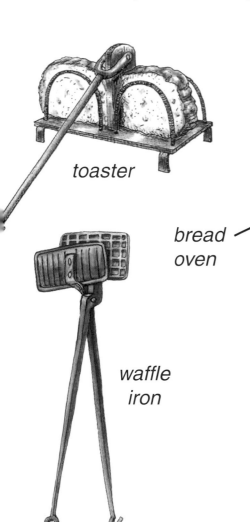

toaster

waffle iron

crane

bread oven

*Food was cooked over an open fire in a fireplace. A **crane** held pots above the fire. Breads and cakes were baked in a bread oven.*

Keeping food fresh

Today, our food comes from many places, such as Asia, South America, and Africa, which are all very far away. Food is transported in ships, airplanes, and trucks. It is refrigerated, frozen, or canned so it will not go bad. When the food arrives at a supermarket, it is kept cold or frozen. After people buy the food, they also store it in their refrigerator to keep it fresh.

Dangerous food

*Without refrigeration, **bacteria** can spoil food quickly and make us sick. How is food safer now than long ago?*

Before refrigeration

Before electricity, people did not have refrigerators to keep food fresh, nor did they have canned food. They did have ways to keep their food from going bad, but it was a challenge, especially during the summer months.

A **smokehouse** was used to flavor meat such as ham and make it last longer.

A **springhouse** was built over a cold-water spring. Milk and other foods were kept in the water so they would not spoil.

Fruit and some vegetables were preserved in jars so they would last for months.

Vegetables that were **pickled**, or preserved in vinegar, lasted longer.

In winter, food was stored in a **root cellar** dug into the cool ground.

The best foods

Long ago, people ate **whole foods**, which are real foods that have not had things taken out or added to them. Modern ways of preparing food often take out the parts that are good for us. Many people are returning to the old, more healthy ways of preparing food. Past ways of farming that do not use **pesticides** and drugs are being practiced again. More people are also eating foods grown close to home, as they did long ago. When food does not have to be transported, there is less air **pollution**.

whole-wheat bread

garden-fresh vegetables

Learn more

Books

Flatt, Lizann. *Life in a Farming Community* (Learn about Rural Life). Crabtree Publishing, 2010.

Hewitt, Sally. *Your Food* (Green Team). Crabtree Publishing, 2009.

Kalman, Bobbie. *I can write a book about how to be healthy and happy* (I can write a book). Crabtree Publishing, 2013.

Kalman, Bobbie. *Where does our food come from?* (My World). Crabtree Publishing, 2011.

Kalman, Bobbie. *Farm Animals* (My World). Crabtree Publishing, 2011.

Kalman, Bobbie. (Kid Power series). Crabtree Publishing, 2003–2004.

Kalman, Bobbie and Lynda Hale. Pioneer Recipes (Historic Communities). Crabtree Publishing, 2001

Kalman, Bobbie. *In the Barn* (Historic Communities). Crabtree Publishing, 1997.

Kalman, Bobbie. *The General Store* (Historic Communities). Crabtree Publishing, 1997.

Kalman, Bobbie. *The Kitchen* (Historic Communities). Crabtree Publishing, 1993.

Peppas, Lynn. *Vehicles on the Farm* (Vehicles on the Move). Crabtree Publishing, 2011.

Websites

This video provides information on farming long ago and today:
www.youtube.com/watch?v=BC5rFsSWM_Q

Learn more about the history of farming from this video:
www.neok12.com/php/watch.php?v=zX585b7b7173 0b4a5c587859&t=Agriculture

See if you know what foods come from plants and which come from animals at:
www.foodafactoflife.org.uk/Activity.aspx?siteId=14 &sectionId=63&contentId=173

Words to know

Note: Some boldfaced words are defined where they appear in the book.

bacteria Tiny organisms that cause food to go bad and cause diseases in animals and people

cider A drink made from freshly pressed apples

crops Plants grown for food

factory A building or group of buildings where things are made

free range Describing a way of farming that allows animals to roam freely and to be raised naturally

grains The seeds of cereal plants, such as wheat, rice, corn, or oats

ingredients A mixture of things that make up foods or recipes

nectar A sweet liquid found in flowers

pesticide A chemical used to kill insects or other pests

pollution Harmful materials that damage the air, water, or soil

preserve To prepare or keep food in a way that will prevent it from spoiling

product Something that is made or created, such as cereal or candy

root cellar A room built underground, which was used to preserve food

sap The liquid that flows through a plant, such as a maple tree

Index